Grade Three

GW00775776

Classical Guitar Playing

Compiled and edited by
Tony Skinner and Raymond Burley

Printed and bound in Great Britain

Published by Registry Publications

Registry Mews, 11-13 Wilton Rd, Bexhill, Sussex, TN40 1HY

Cover guitars: Rohan Lowe, John Price, Martin Fleeson

A CIP record for this publication is available from the British Library
ISBN: 1-898466-63-7

Compiled for **LCM Exams** by

INTRODUCTION

This publication is part of a progressive series of ten handbooks, primarily intended for candidates considering taking the London College Of Music examinations in classical guitar playing. However, given each handbook's wide content of musical repertoire, and associated educational material, the series provides a solid foundation of musical education for any classical guitar student – whether intending to take an examination or not. Whilst the handbooks can be used for independent study, they are ideally intended as a supplement to individual or group tuition.

Examination entry

An examination entry form is provided at the rear of each handbook. This is the only valid entry form for the London College Of Music classical guitar examinations. Please note that *if the entry form is detached and lost, it will not be replaced under any circumstances* and the candidate will be required to obtain a replacement handbook to obtain another entry form.

Editorial information

All performance pieces should be played in full, including all repeats shown. The pieces have been edited specifically for examination use, with all non-required repeat markings omitted. Examination performances must be from this handbook edition. Tempos, fingering, and dynamic markings are for general guidance only and need not be rigidly adhered to.

Right-hand fingering is normally shown on the stem side of the notes:
p = thumb; *i* = index; *m* = middle; *a* = third.

Left-hand fingering is shown with the numbers 1 2 3 4, normally to the left side of the note head.
0 indicates an open string.

String numbers are shown in a circle, normally below the note. For example, ⑥ = 6th string.

Finger shifts are indicated by a small horizontal dash before the left hand finger number.
For example, 2   followed by -2   indicates that the 2nd finger can stay on the same string but move to another fret as a *guide finger*. The finger shift sign should not be confused with a *slide* or *glissando* (where a longer dash joins two noteheads).

Slurs are indicated by a curved line between two notes of differing pitch. These should not be confused with *ties* (where two notes of the *same* pitch are joined by a curved line in order to increase the duration of the first note).

Full barrés (covering 5 or 6 strings with the first finger) are shown by a capital **B**, followed by a Roman numeral to indicate the fret position of the barré. For example, BI indicates a full barré at the first fret. A dotted line will indicate the duration for which the barré should be held.

Half barrés (covering 2 to 4 strings) are shown like this: ½B, followed by a Roman numeral to indicate the fret position of the half barré. For example, ½BI indicates a half barré at the first fret.

Acknowledgements

The editors acknowledge the help of the many libraries and copyright owners that facilitated access to original manuscripts, source materials and facsimiles. The editors are grateful for the advice and support of all the members of the Registry Of Guitar Tutors 'Classical Guitar Advisory Panel', and are particularly indebted for the expertise and contributions of:

Carlos Bonell Hon.RCM, Chris Ackland GRSM LRAM LTCL,
Chaz Hart LRAM, Frank Bliven BM MA, Alan J. Brown LTCL.

SECTION ONE – FINGERBOARD KNOWLEDGE

A maximum of 15 marks may be awarded in this section of the examination. The examiner may ask you to play *from memory* any of the scales, arpeggios or chords shown on the following pages.

Scales and arpeggios must be played *ascending and descending*, i.e. from the lowest note to the highest and back again, without a pause and without repeating the top note. *Apoyando* (rest strokes) or *tirando* (free strokes) can be used, providing a good tone is produced.

Chords should be played *ascending only*, and sounded string by string, starting with the lowest root note. To achieve a legato (i.e. smooth and over-ringing) sound, the whole chord shape should be placed on the fingerboard before, and kept on during, playing. Chords should *always* be played tirando, i.e. using free strokes.

To allow for flexibility in teaching and playing approaches, all the fingering suggestions within this handbook are *not* compulsory and alternative systematic fingerings, that are musically effective, will be accepted.

Suggested tempos are for general guidance only. Slightly slower or faster performances will be acceptable providing that the tempo is maintained evenly throughout. Overall, the examiner will be listening, and awarding marks, for accuracy, evenness and clarity.

Recommended right hand fingering and tempo

Scales:	alternating *im* or *ma*	84 minim beats per minute
Arpeggios:	*pimaima* (reverse descending)	66 minim beats per minute
Chords:	*p* on all bass strings *ima* on treble strings	132 minim beats per minute

---

Key Study

The Key Study links the introduction of a new key to the performance of a short melodic theme from a piece by a well-known composer. The purpose is to make the learning of scales relevant to practical music-making and therefore memorable, as well as providing the opportunity to play music outside the standard guitar repertoire.

The examiner may request you to play any, or all, of the scales within the key study. The examiner will also ask for a performance of ONE of the melodic themes of your choice.

Tempo marking and fingering are for guidance only and need not be rigidly adhered to, providing a good musical performance is produced. The examiner will be listening, and awarding marks, for evidence of melodic phrasing and shaping, as well as for accuracy and clarity.

The Key Study must be played entirely from memory.

E Chromatic scale - 1 octave

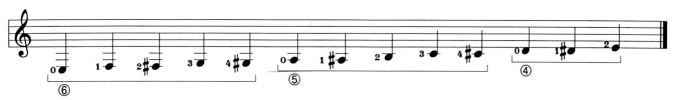

D Melodic Minor scale - 1 octave

A Melodic Minor scale - 2 octaves

E Major scale - 2 octaves

E Major arpeggio - 2 octaves   A Minor arpeggio - 2 octaves

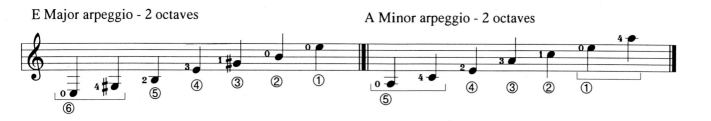

C Major Barré chord   F Major Barré chord   G Major Barré chord

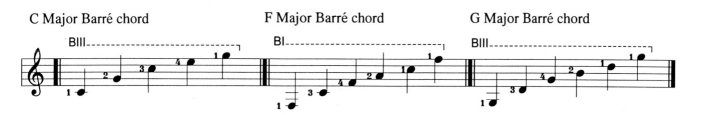

Key Study

The examiner will request a selection of the scales below,
plus ONE melodic theme of the *candidate's choice*.

Bb Major scale - 2 octaves

G Harmonic Minor scale - 2 octaves

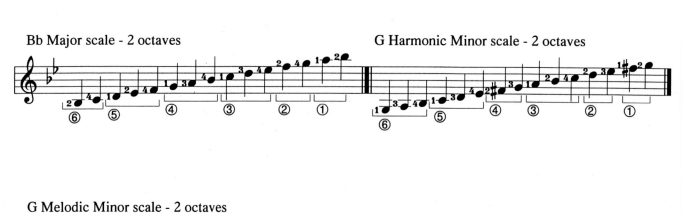

G Melodic Minor scale - 2 octaves

Melodic theme - Option One

Alla Hornpipe
From Water Music

George Frideric Handel
(1685 - 1759)

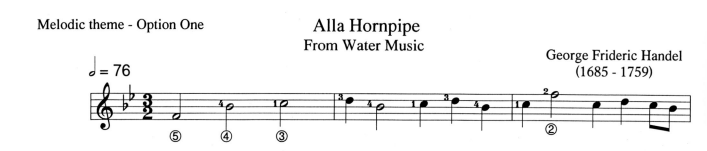

6

Melodic theme - Option Two

Largo
From Symphonie No. 9 Op.95

Antonin Dvorák
(1841 - 1904)

SECTION TWO – PERFORMANCE

Candidates should play any *one* piece from *each* of the three groups. A maximum of 60 marks may be awarded in this section of the examination – i.e. up to 20 marks for each performance.

Fingering, tempo and dynamic markings are for general guidance only and do not need to be adhered to strictly. All repeat markings should be followed.

Performance Tips

Mistris Winter's Jump *(Dowland):*

- This is a dance piece, originally written for lute. To capture the style of the piece it is important to maintain an even tempo throughout, and give due attention to the timing of the many dotted notes which give the piece its distinctive rhythmic character.

- A full barré is required to play the chords in bars 3 and 13. To ensure clarity, make sure that the first finger that forms the barré is positioned flat and straight and as close to the fret as possible.

Allemanda *(Calvi):*

- This piece was originally written for baroque guitar in 1646, although it is based on a melody from an even earlier period – with the first known lute arrangement being 40 years earlier. A steady flowing rhythm is needed to capture the style of the piece.

- Despite the lack of key signature, this piece has a D minor tonality: the notes within the piece can all be found within the D melodic minor scale. Take care to notice where accidentals do, and do not, appear – so as to distinguish between B♭ and B natural notes, and between C and C# notes.

Aria *(Logy):*

- This piece in A minor is written in two clear parts. Care should be taken to ensure that each voice is allowed to sound clearly, with notes ringing for their full value.

- The piece involves several changes from first to third position, such as at the start of bar 2 and in bar 7. These shifts of position should be executed as cleanly as possible. The end of the piece features an inverted mordent, which has been notated for the purposes of clarity; these last three notes could be slurred if preferred.

Larghetto *(Sor):*

- Observe the lower voice rests that occur in bars 2, 4, 10 and elsewhere, as these will help define the phrasing.

- The grace notes that occur in bars 15 and 19 should be played as slurs. To ensure that the piece is learnt with the correct timing, it may be easier to omit these ornaments until the rest of the piece is learnt.

Allegretto *(Carcassi):*

- This piece is in the key of E major – so remember that all F, G, C and D notes have to be sharpened throughout (unless cancelled by a natural sign). An *accidental* A# note also frequently occurs.

- Optional editorial slurs have been added to enable the opening four semiquavers to be played by picking just the first note. Care needs to be taken to ensure that they all sound clearly and evenly.

Ejercicio *(Ferrer):*

- A warm tone and some subtle use of rubato can be employed to capture the lyrical mood of the first section of this piece.

- In the second section (from bar 17 onwards) the repeated open B string is just there to provide a sense of movement and harmonic contrast: the melody lies in the bass, which should be brought out clearly by playing with the thumb.

Poem *(Benham):*

- The composer suggests that "this piece should be approached in a relaxed way, feeling for the phrases implied in the music and avoiding a strict mechanical beat".

- It is recommended that the first note in each bar, apart from the last four bars, should be played with a right hand apoyando stroke to give emphasis and help the upper melodic line stand out from the accompanying arpeggio figures. Care should be taken to give these initial first beat notes their full value. The right hand fingering shown is designed to avoid the immediate repetition of the same finger.

November Morn *(Skinner):*

- This piece should start with a clear bright tone and be performed with a steady pulse; not too much rubato should be used until later in the piece (from around bar 13 onwards).

- The *D.C. al Coda* marking indicates that after bar 19 the piece should be repeated from the beginning until the end of bar 6, before proceeding straight to the *Coda* (which forms the final 2 bars).

A Romantic Interlude *(Breame):*

- The performance direction 'with warmth' gives an idea of the overall feel of the piece, and care should be taken with regard to dynamics. Take note of the *rit.* in bar 9 and the gradual *rall.* in bar 24.

- This piece has a D minor key signature. As well as the C# accidentals, watch out for the frequently recurring B natural notes throughout the piece.

Mistris Winter's Jump

[Group A]

John Dowland
(1563 - 1626)

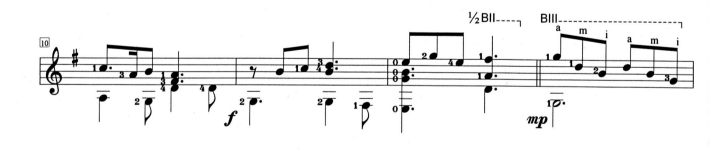

10

Allemanda

[Group A]

Carlo Calvi
(1612 - 1669)

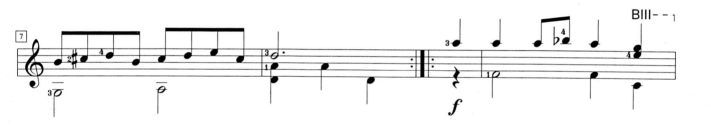

11

Aria

[Group A]

Johann Anton Logy
(1650 - 1721)

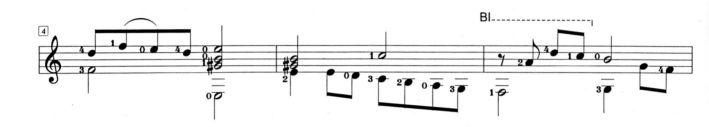

12

Larghetto Op.35 No.3

[Group B]

Fernando Sor
(1778 - 1839)

Allegretto Op.21 No.9

[Group B]

Matteo Carcassi
(1792 - 1853)

14

Ejercicio (Vals)

[Group B]

José Ferrer
(1835 - 1916)

15

Poem

[Group C]

Patrick Benham
(1940 –)

16

November Morn

[Group C]

Tony Skinner
(1960 –)

A Romantic Interlude

[Group C]

Justin Breame
(1972 –)

SECTION THREE – MUSICAL KNOWLEDGE

A maximum of 7 marks may be awarded in this section of the examination. The examiner will ask questions, based on the music performed, to test the candidate's knowledge of basic rudiments of music including the value of notes and rests, numerical value of intervals, key and time signatures. The examiner will also expect an understanding of any terms and signs that appear in the music performed. The information below provides a summary of what is required.

The clef and stave

Treble Clef   E   F   G   A   B   C   D   E   F   G   A   B   C   D   E   F   G   A   B   C

Leger lines are used to extend the range of notes above and below the stave.
The treble clef is also known as the *G clef* – since it is drawn looped around the G line.

Notes and rests
The table below shows the names of the notes and rests, and their values.

Traditional name	Modern name	Note	Rest	Value in crotchet beats
semibreve	whole note			4
dotted minim	dotted half note			3
minim	half note			2
dotted crotchet	dotted quarter note			1½
crotchet	quarter note			1
dotted quaver	dotted eighth note			¾
quaver	eighth note			½
semiquaver	16th note			¼
demisemiquaver	32nd note			⅛

an *acciaccatura* (grace note). This ornamental note should be played as quickly as possible on the main beat – i.e. 'squeezed in' before the principal note is heard.

Groups of two or more grace notes are normally beamed together, with the diagonal stroke through the stem omitted. They should be played as quickly as possible before the main note.

Dots and ties

A dot after a note increases the value of that note by half of its original value. For example, a *dotted crotchet* is equivalent to 3 quavers in length, whereas a normal crotchet is equivalent to 2 quavers in length.

The value of a note may also be increased by the use of a *tie*. Only the first note is played, but it is held on for its own length plus that of the following tied note. So the tied note in the example below lasts for the equivalent of 3 quavers.

dotted crotchet   tie

Major and minor key signatures

| Bb Major or G Minor | F Major or D Minor | C Major or A Minor | G Major or E Minor | D Major or B Minor | A Major or F# Minor | E Major or C# Minor |

A sharp, flat or natural that appears during a piece of music, rather than as part of the key signature, is called an *accidental*. It has the effect of sharpening or flattening just that one note, and any others at the same pitch within the same bar. It does not affect notes in the remaining bars.

Candidates should be able to identify whether a piece is in the major key or its relative minor key. This is often indicated by the presence of an accidental on the leading note of the minor key. For example, G# in the key of A minor, D# in E minor, and C# in D minor. Candidates should also examine the first and final chord, or bass note, to help establish the tonality.

Intervals

Candidates will be expected to identify by numeric value (e.g. 3rd, 6th) any interval within the range of an octave that occurs in the music performed. Examples in the key of C major are given below.

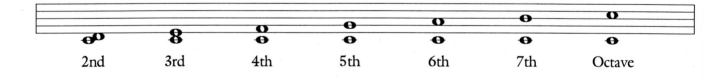

2nd   3rd   4th   5th   6th   7th   Octave

You can work out any interval number by counting the number of lines and spaces between two notes – making sure to include the first and final notes of the interval in your count.

Time signatures

The time signatures that occur at this grade are:

$\frac{2}{4}$ = 2 crotchet beats per bar, (a). Also known as *simple duple time*.

$\frac{3}{4}$ = 3 crotchet beats per bar, (b). *Simple triple time*.

$\frac{4}{4}$ = 4 crotchet beats per bar, (c). This is also indicated by $\mathbf{C}$, (d). *Simple quadruple time*.

$\frac{3}{8}$ = 3 quaver beats per bar, (e). *Simple triple time*.

$\frac{6}{8}$ = 6 quavers, but with 2 dotted crotchet beats per bar, (f). *Compound duple time*.

$\frac{3}{2}$ = 3 minim beats per bar, (g). *Simple triple time*.

(a)   (b)   (c)   (d)   (e)   (f)   (g)

Common terms and signs

Candidates should should have an understanding of any terms and signs that appear in the music performed. Some examples are given below.

>	accent
⌢·	fermata (pause sign): hold the note longer than usual
,	comma: indicates the end of a phrase, and suggests a slight breath
D.C. al Coda	repeat from the beginning up to the sign ⏀ , then go straight to the *Coda*
D.S. al Coda	repeat from the sign 𝄋 , and play up to the sign ⏀ , then go straight to the *Coda*
D.C. al Fine	repeat from the beginning up to the point marked *Fine* (the end)
sim.	*simile*: continue in a like manner

Tenuto sign – note to be held for its full value and slightly emphasised.

Staccato dot – note to be played short and detached.

Repeat sign.
(Play from the previous 2 vertical dots, or, in their absence, from the beginning.)

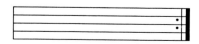

First time ending.
(On the first playing, play the notes below this box.)

Second time ending.
(On the second playing, omit the first time ending and play from this bar.)

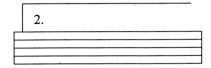

Dynamics

ppp	*pp*	*p*	*mp*	*mf*	*f*	*ff*	*fff*
pianissimo very soft	*piano* soft	*mezzo-piano* medium soft	*mezzo-forte* medium loud	*forte* loud		*fortissimo* very loud	

crescendo – getting louder

decrescendo – getting softer

dim (diminuendo)   gradually becoming softer

Tempo terms

Rall. (rallentando)	becoming gradually slower
Rit. (ritenuto)	held back
poco rit.	held back a little
a tempo	in time, i.e. return to normal speed after a deviation
♩ = 120	metronome marking (e.g. 120 crotchet beats per minute)
Allegro	at a fast and lively pace
Allegretto	fairly fast (not as fast as *Allegro*)
Larghetto	not quite as slow as *Largo*
Largo	slow and stately

Candidates should also refer to the Introduction of this handbook which outlines the meaning of the specialist guitar signs.

SECTION FOUR – PLAYING AT SIGHT

The examiner will show you the sight reading test and allow you just a short time to look over it before performing it. The table below shows the range of the piece:

Length	Keys	Time signatures	Note values	Fingerboard positions
4 bars	Major: F, C, G, D Minor: D, A, E, B	2 3 4 6 4 4 4 8	o 𝅗𝅥. 𝅗𝅥 ♩. ♩ ♪♪	1st / 2nd

PERFORMANCE TIPS

1. Always check the key and time signature BEFORE you start to play.

2. Once you have identified the key it is helpful to remember that the notes will all come from the key scale.

3. Before you start to play, quickly scan through the piece and check any notes or rhythms that you are unsure of. Where fretted bass notes occur simultaneously with melody notes, decide which left-hand fingering you will need to use.

4. Note the tempo or style marking, but be careful not to play at a tempo at which you cannot maintain accuracy throughout.

5. Once you start to play, try and keep your eyes on the music. Avoid the temptation to keep looking at the fingerboard – that's a sure way to lose your place in the music.

6. If you do make an error, try not to let it affect your confidence for the rest of the piece. It is better to keep going and capture the overall shape of the piece, rather than stopping and going back to correct errors.

The following examples show the *type* of pieces that will be presented in the examination.

(i) Lento

(ii) Andantino

(iii) Vivace

(iv) Andante

(v) Allegretto

(vi) Moderato

SECTION FIVE – AURAL AWARENESS

A maximum of 8 marks may be awarded in this section of the examination. The tests will be played by the examiner on either guitar or piano, at the examiner's discretion. The examples below are shown in guitar notation and give a broad indication of the type of tests that will be given during the examination. Candidates wishing to view the piano notation for these tests should obtain the London College Of Music *Sample Ear Tests* booklet.

Rhythm tests

1. The examiner will play a short piece of music in $^6_8$ time, similar to the examples below. The candidate should beat in time (as in 2 in a bar) with a clear beat, in time with the examiner's playing.

> To beat in 2 time, begin with your arm out in front of you, with your hand at eye level. The first beat of each bar should be shown by a strong downwards motion of the arm and the second beat by a return upwards to your starting position.

2. The examiner will show the candidate a sheet (similar to the example below) containing a number of common $^6_8$ rhythm patterns. The examiner will then play one or more of these patterns from one line; the candidate being informed which line. The candidate should tell the examiner which patterns were played.

Pitch tests

1. The examiner will play two notes together, which will be not more than a perfect fifth apart. The candidate should identify the interval between the two notes by number, e.g. 2nd, 3rd, 4th or 5th.

If preferred, the candidate can play the higher note of an interval back on the guitar – the key having been named, the tonic chord sounded and the higher note of the interval having been played by the examiner. The first note played by the candidate will be taken as the response. The examiner may conduct this test twice with two different intervals.

Four examples of what the examiner might play in both tests are given below.

Option 1.

Option 2.

2. The examiner will play a phrase up to three bars in length, in either a major or minor key. The candidate should sing back the phrase after the key is stated and the tonic chord sounded. The range of keys will be limited to C G D F and B♭ major and A and E minor. The examiner will select a suitable octave according to the age and gender of the candidate. If preferred, the candidate can play back the phrase on the guitar.

Here are three examples:

London College of **Music** & **Media**
THAMES VALLEY UNIVERSITY

Examination Entry Form
for
Classical Guitar

GRADE THREE
or Leisure Play Transitional

PLEASE COMPLETE CLEARLY IN INK AND IN BLOCK CAPITAL LETTERS

SESSION (Spring/Summer/Winter): _____ YEAR: _____

Preferred Examination Centre (if known): _____
If left blank you will examined at the nearest venue to your home address.

Candidate Details:
Candidate Name (as to appear on certificate):

_____

Address: _____

_____ Postcode: _____

Tel. No. (day): _____ (evening): _____

Tick this box if you are also entering for LCM Theory of Music ☐
If so, which Grade? _____

Teacher Details:
Teacher Name (as to appear on certificate): _____

LCM Teacher Code (if entered previously): _____

RGT Tutor Code (if applicable): _____

Address: _____

_____ Postcode: _____

Tel. No. (day): _____ (evening): _____

Tick this box if any details above have changed since your last LCM entry ☐

Tick this box if the teacher has also entered pupils for ☐
RGT Electric or Bass Guitar examinations for the same session.

IMPORTANT NOTES

- It is the candidate's responsibility to have knowledge of, and comply with, the current syllabus requirements. Where candidates are entered for examinations by a teacher, the teacher must take responsibility that candidates are entered in accordance with the current syllabus requirements. Failure to carry out any of the examination requirements may lead to disqualification.
- For candidates with special needs, a letter giving details, and medical certificate as appropriate, should be attached.
- Any practical appointment requests (e.g. 'prefer morning,' or 'prefer weekdays') must be made at the time of entry. **LCM and its Representatives will take note of the information given, however, no guarantees can be made that all wishes will be met.**
- Submission of this entry is an undertaking to abide by the current regulations as listed in the current syllabus and any subsequent regulations updates published in the LCM Examinations Newsletter issued each term.
- Entries for public centres should be sent **to the LCM local representative.** Contact the LCM office for details of your nearest centre or to enquire about setting up your own centre.

Examination Fee   £ _____

Late Entry Fee (if necessary)   £ _____

Total amount submitted   £ _____
Cheques or postal orders should be made payable to **'Thames Valley University'.**

A current list of fees and entry deadlines is available from LCM Exams.

LCM Exams
Thames Valley University
St Mary's Road
London
W5 5RF

Tel: 020 8231 2364
Fax: 020 8231 2433

e-mail: lcm.exams@tvu.ac.uk

The standard LCM music entry form is NOT valid for Classical Guitar entries. **Entry to the examination is only possible via this original form. Photocopies of this form will not be accepted under any circumstances.**

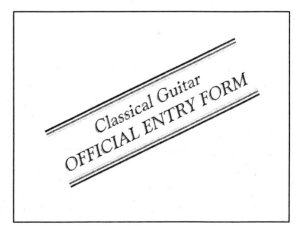